A NEW AND BETTER *YOU*

Written by Joe Harbot

26 June – 14 July 2018
The Yard Theatre

Cast

Alex Austin
Saffron Coomber
Hannah Traylen
Amber Cargill
Lara-Ann Goldbourne
Ariana Williams

Credits

Writer	Joe Harbot
Director	Cheryl Gallacher
Designer	Bethany Wells
Lighting Designer	Jess Bernberg
Composer and Sound Designer	Josh Anio Grigg
Movement Director	Seke Chimutengwende
Assistant Director and Chaperone	Lizzie Manwaring
Casting Director	Ruth O'Dowd CDG
Stage Manager on The Book	Katie Bachtler
Production Manager	Jack Greenyer
Production Electrician	Philip Burke
Video Engineer	Ian Syme
Assistant Stage Manager	Rachel Stinton

First produced by The Yard Theatre.

The first production of *A New and Better You* was supported by Arts Council England, the Fidelio Charitable Trust, Royal Victoria Hall Foundation and Schroder Charity Trust.

Supported using public funding by
**ARTS COUNCIL
ENGLAND**

Alex Austin

Theatre credits include: *Gundog, Grimly Handsome, Primetime, Yen, Pigeons* (Royal Court), *Thebes Land* (Arcola), *Fury* (Soho Theatre), *Barbarians* (Bad Physics/Young Vic), *The Skriker* (Royal Exchange), *Henry The Fifth, The Nutcracker, The Man With The Disturbingly Smelly Foot, How to Think the Unthinkable* (Unicorn Theatre), *Idomeneus* (The Gate Theatre), *Hope, Light and Nowhere (Underbelly)*, *My City* (Almeida Theatre), *Telling Tales* and *Encourage the Others* (Almeida Young Friends).

Film, television and radio credits include: *Blood Out of a Stone* (Watersmeet Productions/BFI Flare), *Legacy* (Legacy Films), *The Christmas Candle* (Pinewood Films), *The Hooligan Factory* (Altitude HF Ltd), *The World's End* (Black Pictures Lts), *The Swarm* (Stray Bear Productions), *Liar* (brocess Ltd), *Sherlock* (Hartswood), *The Interceptor, New Tricks, The Musketeers, Holby City* (BBC), *Misfits,* (Clerkenwell Films) and *Ancient Greek* (BBC Radio 4).

Saffron Coomber

Film credits include: *Electricity* (Stone City Films), *Dustbin Baby* (BBC).

Television credits include: *Cuffs,* (Tiger Aspect/BBC One), *Eastenders, Youngers, Holby City, Tracy Beaker Returns (series 1-3), Doctors* (BBC), *Runaway* (CBBC) and *The Bill* (Talkback Thames).

A New and Better You is Saffron's professional theatre debut.

Hannah Traylen

Professional theatre credits include: *Heroine* (HighTide). Theatre credits while training include: *Coram Boy, The Libertine, Time and The Conways, Oliver Twist, Three Sisters, Twelfth Night* (Italia Conti) and *God Bless Ye Merry Gentlemen* (Grindstone, Tristan Bates Theatre).

Television credits include: *Howards End* (BBC/Starz), *Doctors* (BBC), *Harlots* (ITV Encore), *Call the Midwife* (BBC) and *Unforgotten* (ITV).

Amber Cargill

Amber Jade Nixon Cargill aged 8 is a bubbly and friendly girl who loves to help others. Amber is just starting out in the worlds of modelling, acting and singing but is keen to progress and develop her professional skills. Amber loves recite her favourite lines from famous films and theatre productions, old and new. Amber recently participated in ger first catwalk show which she enjoyed fiercely, strutting down the catwalk and striking a perfect pose.

A New and Better You is Amber's professional theatre debut.

Lara-Ann Goldbourne

Lara-Ann has performed in the Passion Dance Academy biannnual production of *Famous* at the Beck Theatre, and was part of the Passion Dance Academy's 'Elite' competition team. In 2017 Lara-Ann starred in The British Theatre Academy's summer production of *The Adventures of Pinocchio* at the Ambassador Theatre (West End). Lara also performed in RARE Productions' *Hairspray* at the Wyllyotts Theatre Potters Bar and *Grease* at the Theatre Royal Windsor.

Lara-Ann has attended Pineapple Performing Arts School since September and will be performing in their show in July. Lara-Ann also attend Disney's Lion King Cub School.

Lara -Ann has decided this is what she wanted to do with her life and works extremely hard to fulfil her dream. Teachers say she is a star pupil and can't wait to see her name in lights in years to come.

A New and Better You is Lara-Ann's professional theatre debut.

Ariana Williams

Ariana Williams is 9 years old and lives with her family in Kent. Since 2017 Ariana has attended All the Arts Theatre School, where she develops her dancing, singing and acting skills. Ariana has performed in several festivals arranged by All the Arts Theatre School as well as end of season productions including Disney Descendants, in which she played the lead role of Mona.

In addition to acting, singing and dancing Ariana loves gymnastics and cooking and loves watching cookery shows. Ariana is excited about her first appearance in *A New and Better You* with The Yard Theatre and thanks everyone for giving her this opportunity.

A New and Better You is Ariana's professional theatre debut.

Joe Harbot
Writer

Joe Harbot is a graduate of the Royal Court Writers' Programme and has had work performed at the Royal Court, Young Vic, Soho Theatre and Southwark Playhouse. He has worked with a number of new writing theatre companies, including Headlong, Paines Plough and Nabokov. His first play, *The Boy on the Swing*, was staged at Live Theatre Newcastle, directed by Jeremy Herrin, and again at The Arcola in 2011, and his play *Potholes* was shown at Theatre 503 and was longlisted for the Bruntwood Prize for Playwriting 2013 and 2018.

Cheryl Gallacher
Director

Cheryl is an Artistic Associate of the Yard. She was Co-Director of TheatreState, an Associate Company of Exeter Bikeshed and Camden People's Theatre between 2012-2016, and work included *Tribute Acts* (UK Tour) and, *The Fanny Hill Project* (Camden People's Theatre, Exeter Bikeshed). As a director, her work includes *Chapel Street* by Luke Barnes (The Bush, Underbelly, Old Red Lion) and she has devised work with young people for theatres including The Almeida and The Yard, as well as the live installation *An Alternative London* with members of Crisis at the National Theatre.

Bethany Wells
Designer

Trained in architecture, Bethany is a performance designer working across dance, theatre and installation, with a particular interest in site-specific and devised performance. Bethany is interested in design as a form of activism, and works to explore what can be achieved politically and socially by the collective live experience of performance. Bethany is an Associate Artist with Middle Child Theatre, Hull.

Recent work includes: *Journey With Absent Friends* (Grief Series), *Legacy* (York Theatre Royal), *TRUST* (Gate Theatre), *Party Skills for the End of the World* (Nigel Barrett and Louise Mari), *The Department of Distractions* (Third Angel), *All We Ever Wanted Was Everything* (Middle Child), *Cosmic Scallies* (Graeae + Royal Exchange), *We Were Told There Was Dancing* (Royal Exchange Young Company), *Removal Men* (The Yard Theatre), *Dark Corners* (Polar Bear), *Seen and Not Heard* (Complicite Creative Learning), *The Desire Paths* (Third Angel), *The Factory* (Royal Exchange Young Company), *THE FUTURE* (Company 3), *Late Night Love* (Eggs Collective), *Live Art Dining* (Live

Art Bistro), *Race Cards* (Selina Thompson), *Correspondence* (Old Red Lion Theatre), *Partus* (Third Angel), *My Eyes Went Dark* (Finborough Theatre) and *WINK* (Theatre 503).

An ongoing project, WARMTH, is a wood-fired mobile sauna and performance space, commissioned by Compass Live Art and touring nationally.

Josh Anio Grigg
Composer and Sound Designer

Josh Anio Grigg is a producer, sound designer and artist from London. Being born under the sign of Aquarius blesses him with the ability to be original, independant and progressive, although he can run from emotional expression and be prone to stubbornness. The rising Taurus sign can make Josh very earthy, practical and sensuous. Josh completed a Drama,Theatre and Performance degree at Roehampton University of Surrey in 2008. He has designed sound for many spaces across London as well as creating and performing music in festivals across Europe.

Jess Bernberg
Lighting Designer

Jess is a graduate of Guildhall School of Music and Drama and the 2018 Laboratory Associate Lighting Designer at Nuffield Southampton Theatres. She received the Association of Lighting Designer's Francis Reid Award in 2017.

Recent designs include: *The Marbleous Route Home* (Young Vic), *Reactor* (Arts Ed), *Sisterhood* (Marlborough Theatre), *Dungeness, Love and Information* (Nuffield Southampton Theatres), *Buggy Baby* (The Yard Theatre), *Devil with the Blue Dress, FCUK'D* (Off West End Award nomination), (The Bunker), *Split, WAYWARD* (Vaults), *Ajax* (The Space), *The Blue Hour of Natalie Barney, The Dowager's Oyster, Youkali: The Pursuit of Happiness, The Selfish Giant* (Arcola Theatre), *The Death of Ivan Ilyich* (Merton Arts Space), *And the Rest of Me Floats* (Birmingham Rep), *And Here I Am* (UK Tour, Co-Design with Andy Purves), *The Poetry We Make* (Vaults Festival/RADA/Rosemary Branch/Old Red Lion), *This is Matty, and He is Fucked* (Winemaker's Club), *Flux: Shadowlines* (King's Place), *SQUIRM* (King's Head/Theatre 503/Bread & Roses Theatre/C Venues), *Glitter & Tears* (Bread & Roses Theatre/theSpace UK), *Balm in Gilead, The Same Deep Water As Me, August* (Guildhall).

As Assistant Lighting Designer: *A Streetcar Named Desire* (Nuffield Southampton Theatres), *A Tale of Two Cities* (Regent's Park Open Air Theatre), *Fox on the Fairway* (Queen's Theatre Hornchurch).

Seke Chimutengwende
Movement Director

Seke Chimutengwende works in dance as a performer, choreographer and teacher. He has performed with companies such as DV8 Physical Theatre, Lost Dog and Fabulous Beast, and in gallery based works by Trisha Brown and Tino Sehgal as well as with numerous independent choreographers. For his own company Seke Chimutengwende & Friends he has choreographed four works including *The Time Travel Piece* for The Place Prize 2012 and *King Arthur*, which premiered at The Yard Theatre in 2015. Seke's current choreographic project, *Black Holes,* is a duet made in collaboration with Alexandrina Hemsley exploring Afrofuturism. Since 2006, Seke has performed over 60 improvised solos internationally and has performed ensemble improvisation with Neat Timothy since 2009. Seke is currently a guest lecturer in improvisation at London Contemporary Dance School, The Rambert School of Ballet & Contemporary Dance, Central School of Speech and Drama and Goldsmiths University.

Lizzie Manwaring
Assistant Director and Chaperone

Lizzie is a recent graduate of Queen Mary, University of London. Recent directing credits include: *The Woman Who Gave Birth To A Goat* (Camden People's Theatre), *WAGGO* (Edinburgh Fringe), *And Then...* (Latitude) and she has worked with companies including Complicite, Goat and Monkey, National Youth Theatre, and Loquitur Theatre.

Ruth O'Dowd CDG
Casting Director

Recent projects include *The Outsider, Love Lies Bleeding and Plays by Lars Norén* (The Print Room), *Jerusalem* (Watermill Theatre), *Ink* (Duke of York's Theatre), *The Grapes of Wrath* (Nuffield Theatre and tour), *My Father Odysseus, Minotaur, The Velveteen Rabbit, Henry the Fifth, Britain's Best Recruiting Sergeant, Caucasian Chalk Circle, The Nutcracker, How Nigeria Became* and *Seesaw* (Unicorn Theatre).

As Associate to Anne McNulty CDG: *King Lear* (Duke of York's Theatre), *The Lieutenant of Inishmore* (Noel Coward Theatre), *Red* (Wyndham's Theatre), *What If Women Ruled The World, Fatherland* (Manchester International Festival 2017), *Ink, Bakkhai, Carmen Disruption* (Almeida Theatre), *Forty Years On, The House They Grew Up In, The Country Girls, Someone Who'll Watch Over Me* (Chichester Festival Theatre), *No Man's Land* (Wyndham's Theatre and tour), *Into The Woods* (Royal Exchange, Manchester), *Photograph 51* (Noel Coward Theatre) and *Outside Mullingar* (Ustinov Studio, Bath).

Jack Greenyer
Production Manager

Jack recently completed his final year of the Royal Central School of Speech and Drama's BA Theatre Practice: Technical and Production Management course. He has since been working with theatre companies such as Complicite, National Youth Theatre, Iris Theatre and Big House Theatre Company. Jack continues his commitment to help creative practitioners make the most of their spaces through his work with his company, Infinity Technical & Production Services.

Katie Bachtler
Stage Manager on the Book

Theatre as Company Stage Manager/Stage Manager on Book includes *Grotty* (Damsel Productions, The Bunker, London), *Winter Solstice* (ATC, UK Tour), *Dear Brutus* (Southwark Playhouse), Various Productions (Assembly, The Box, Edinburgh Fringe), *Angels in America II* (New Celts Productions, Edinburgh), *Side Effects* (Poplar Union), *Crude* (Grid Iron, Dundee), *Moon Dog* (Carnegie Hall, Dunfermline). Upcoming work includes *Big Aftermath of a Small Disclosure* (ATC, Summerhall, Edinburgh Fringe) and *Fabric* (Damsel Productions, Soho Theatre). Events include Gibson Street Gala (Glasgow), Kentish Town Community Festival (London), and the Glasgow Film Festival each year as Venue Coordinator. Trained at Edinburgh Stage Management School, and completed an MA in English Literature and Theatre Studies at the University of Glasgow.

In 2011 a group of volunteers, led by Jay Miller, used recycled and reclaimed materials to convert a disused warehouse in Hackney Wick into a theatre, bar and kitchen. They called it The Yard. A multi-award winning theatre, The Yard offers a space for artists to grow new stories and new ideas, and for audiences to access outstanding new work.

"One of London's most essential theatres" **Lyn Gardner, *The Guardian***

The Yard has rapidly established itself as a theatrical necessity with a reputation for upending theatrical traditions, and injecting creativity and fearlessness into wider contemporary culture.

The Yard is committed to:
1. Exposing stories from unheard voices.
2. Interrogating the process of writing for performance.
3. Discovering and developing artists.

In The Yard's short existence it has had significant success. This includes transfers to the National Theatre for *Beyond Caring* and *Chewing Gum Dreams*, and numerous awards including the final Peter Brook Empty Space Award (2017). Success has also led to partnerships with leading theatres and organisations, including recent partners the Young Vic, Royal Court Theatre, the National Theatre and HighTide Festival Theatre.

"The most important theatre in east London" ***Time Out***

Alongside the theatre, The Yard is recognised as one of London's most diverse and exciting venues for experiencing new music, filling the bar with people dancing until the early hours.

Over the last seven years The Yard has become a cornerstone for the Hackney Wick community. Hub67, a neighbouring community centre, is managed by The Yard and is home to The Yard's Local Programme, which connects local residents with the arts. Yard Young Artists is at the heart of this, a programme that gives children and young people aged 4-19 the chance to see theatre, work with dynamic artists and create work for The Yard stage.

The Yard Theatre brings artists and audiences together in an exciting environment where anything becomes possible.

Recent productions include:

Buggy Baby written by Josh Azouz, directed by Ned Bennett (2018), which played a sold-out, critically acclaimed, extended run. ("A theatrical rollercoaster... extraordinary" ★★★★★ *WhatsOnStage*)

This Beautiful Future written by Rita Kalnejais, directed by Jay Miller (2017), was the first show to be remounted at The Yard following a sold-out, critically acclaimed and extended run. ("Nothing short of mesmerising" ★★★★★ *The Stage*)

Removal Men written by M. J. Harding, with Jay Miller (2016), which received two Off West End Award nominations for Best New Play and Most Promising Playwright ("Jay Miller's mesmerically intense production uses music to carve out a space for huge ideas" ★★★★ *Time Out*).

Made Visible written by Deborah Pearson, directed by Stella Odunlami (2016), which sparked lively debate around white privilege ("a serious examination of racism and the inadequacies of liberalism" ★★★★ *The Guardian*).

LINES written by Pamela Carter, directed by Jay Miller (2015), which received substantial critical acclaim ("directed with finesse by The Yard's properly talented artistic director Jay Miller" ★★★★ *Time Out*).

The Mikvah Project written by Josh Azouz (2015), directed by Jay Miller, which played a sold-out, extended run ("Every moment feels rich with meaning" ★★★★ *Time Out*).

Beyond Caring by Alexander Zeldin (2014), which transferred to the National Theatre and has completed an international tour ("quietly devastating" ★★★★ *The Guardian*).

Artistic Director – Jay Miller
Executive Director – Sam Hansford
Finance and Operations Manager – Jack Haynes
Theatre Producer – Ashleigh Wheeler
Marketing and Communications Manager – Alex Krook
Local Producer – Katherine Igoe-Ewer
Assistant Producer – Lara Tysseling
Development Officer – Gareth Cutter

Finance and Administration Assistant – Kellie Grogan

Music and Events Producer- Ben Bishop

Production and Venue Coordinator – Jessica Barter

Theatre Technician – James Dawson

Bar and Venue Manager – Felix Yoosefinjad

Assistant Bar and Venue Manager – Olivia Carr-Archer

Bar Duty Manager – Unique Spencer

Artistic Associates – Josh Azouz, Cheryl Gallacher, Dan Hutton, Gbolahan Obisesan, Greg Wohead

Board – Greg Delaney, Yenny Chong, Antony Gummett, Jay Miller, Ben Rogers, Robin Saphra, Nick Starr, Anna Vaughan, Carolyn Ward

Supporters

 Supported using public funding by **ARTS COUNCIL ENGLAND**

The Kirsh Foundation

 Garfield Weston FOUNDATION

Patrick and Helena Frost Foundation

Thank you to all our Friends & Guardians including:

Francesco Curto & Chantal Rivest

Joanna Kennedy

Greg Delaney

The David Pearlman Charitable Foundation

Ian & Janet Edmondson

Ben Rogers

Laura Hodgson

Robin Saphra

Nicholas Hytner

Anna Vaughan & Dan Fletcher

Melanie Johnson

Archie Ward & Carolyn Ward

Thanks:

Thank you to everyone who has helped us make *A New and Better You*. We couldn't have done it without you.

We would like to thank: Kadine at Hobs Studio, Tom at Plexal, Bianka Nixon, Hannah Williams, Natasha Young, Joshua Miles, Paksie Vernon, Ria Zmitrowicz, Jonathan Haynes at Whitelight, Gemma Rowan and Camden Youth Theatre, Yolanda at the Old Baths, and Kulvinder at Wood Mill Studios and Ben Stephen from The Albany.

Joe Harbot

A NEW AND BETTER YOU

OBERON BOOKS
LONDON

WWW.OBERONBOOKS.COM

First published in 2018 by Oberon Books Ltd
521 Caledonian Road, London N7 9RH
Tel: +44 (0) 20 7607 3637 / Fax: +44 (0) 20 7607 3629
e-mail: info@oberonbooks.com
www.oberonbooks.com

A catalogue record for this book is available from the British
Library.

PB ISBN: 9781786825476
E ISBN: 9781786825483

Cover design: Jelena Luise Schuhmacher

Printed and bound by 4edge Limited, Essex, UK.
eBook conversion by Lapiz Digital Services, India.

May you live in interesting times

May you be recognised by those in high places

May you find what you are looking for

An expanse of desert; you sit in the centre of it.
Everyone has a key around their neck–

You're standing by the bed– not even a full double–

The bed is pressed up against the wardrobe–

The wardrobe is made out of tiny pieces of wood held together with glue– laminated wood pulp–

The clothes inside aren't folded– the clothes aren't ironed–

They're not washed even–

The sky is black outside–

The mirror is broken– how did that happen?

You can hear sirens in the distance–

Everyone else is asleep– asleep in their own diminutive rooms–

Strangers– yes– you live with strangers– even at your age– on the outskirts of the city–

You're not looking after yourself– you're allowing yourself to slip

You're not being mindful of your decisions–

You don't participate in regular exercise–

You remain sitting for extended periods–

You regularly drink over the recommended daily allowance–

You don't eat your five a day–

You're always on your phone– watching videos–

Wasting time–

You play that game with sweets– moving the sweets around–

You can't sleep–

You're only passively engaged with your surroundings–

You've let yourself become a paste–

A dull flavourless mush–

You've failed– totally failed– to shape your life in any
meaningful way–

When I look at you I think– and I'm sure a lot of people think–

What a clear example you are–

What a clear example of what not to be–

Of what to avoid–

What a waste of space

What a dried out husk

It's no good looking at the floor

The floor can't help you

You were born screaming into the world–

Mouth open– full of possibility– full of potential–

Electricity in your nerves–

Oxygen in the blood–

Heart beating–

Lungs expanding–

Synapses firing–

You're standing on this rich dark earth alive–

Alive–!

To be afforded that opportunity–

And to be here–

Like this–

Doing this– doing what–? doing nothing–

Is that what you wanted for yourself?

       No

Is this who you are?

       No

Say it–

       This isn't who I am

Louder–

       This isn't who I am–!

Look at those tracksuit bottoms–

Look at that t-shirt–

When was the last time you washed those?

What's that on the front?

Is that blood?

Is that sauce?

Take them off

Take a look at yourself

Take a long hard look

Is that your body?

Is that the body you want?

Those weak and shapeless arms–

Those turned out knees– the thighs touching–

That waistline– the stretch marks– the soft edges–

The folds around the stomach– the rash under the folds–

The spots on your forehead– the blocked pores generally–

The hyperpigmentation– the large dark nipples– the varicose
veins–

The poor posture– the hunched shoulders– the curved back–

The unaligned hips– the splayed feet–

The long toes– the thickening nails– the cracked heels–

The dead skin–

The distinct aroma– not just from the feet–

From the armpit–

The groin–

The nether regions–

You stink

You're rotting

You're dying–

You're letting it happen–

You're just standing there and letting it happen–

Apathetic–

Pathetic–

Take your underwear off

      I don't want to

Take it off so we can see

Look at those nether regions–

There's no way you can be satisfied with those nether regions–

Those genitals–

Are you–?

Is it really a surprise you can't find anyone willing to touch them–?

Willing to put them in their mouth–?

They're ugly–

They're dirty–

They're poorly maintained–

Proper maintenance is vital–

Yes

People make assessments–

They make assessments in every moment

They make an assessment the moment they meet you

They meet you and they make an instantaneous assessment–

Whether you're worth their effort– their time–

Whether you're worth investing in– personally or otherwise–

And they're right to make an assessment

That's a positive thing to do– to examine and evaluate the world around them–

To enable themselves to make clear-headed decisions about what they want–

About what will help them facilitate that– and what won't–

About what's best for them– and what isn't–

Because naturally they want the best for themselves– don't they?

Yes

They deserve it–

Yes

We all deserve the best we can get for ourselves–

You included– you're not exempt from that–

But it doesn't come on a plate

The world won't fall in your lap

You have to open your eyes–

Be realistic–

Nothing is promised–

Love isn't unconditional–

Nobody owes you any favours–

There's a reason why people pull away– keep their distance–

Recoil when you touch their shoulder– the small of their back–

Close their eyes while you're talking– grit their teeth– hold their breath–

You bring nothing to the table– you've turned up to the party empty handed–

You're the bottom of the barrel– you're the dregs of society

Pond scum

The rancid white foam that collects by the riverbank–

You don't deserve their attention– you haven't earned it–

Would you want to take that clammy palm?

Touch that damp neck?

Converse with that slow brain– that mumble–?

Listen to that laboured breathing?

Would you want to embrace that body?

Lie beside it in the dark–?

Would you want to put your mouth between those legs?

With all that skin around?

Those sad folds?

The hair growing weirdly?

Those odd tufts of hair?

Would you want to partner up with you?

A leech that offers nothing–

A burden on the human species and on the planet–

       No

No–

       No

No–

A large box is brought in and placed on a stand. It is opened with the key from your neck.

Inside the box is a miniature bedroom, exactly as described; dirty, crowded and depressing. You look inside it— it is not a model; it is real.

Your whole life is in here— your waste of space life.

I'm sorry I'm such a waste of space

I'm sorry I can't afford to live on my own

I'm sorry my room is the same length as the bed

I'm sorry my wardrobe is so cheap

I'm sorry my sheets are polyester

I'm sorry I'm prone to periods of deep reflection

To depression

I'm sorry I can't seem to pull myself out of it

I'm sorry I don't have full time employment

I'm sorry I don't have get up and go

I'm sorry I'm not a morning person

I'm sorry I don't like socialising

I'm sorry I'm not interesting

I'm sorry I'm not secure

I'm sorry I'm so passive

I'm sorry I'm overweight

I'm sorry my upbringing wasn't always easy

I'm sorry I use my upbringing as an excuse

I'm sorry I push difficult thoughts down to the bottom of my heart

I'm sorry I'm on the back foot– that my best foot isn't forward–

I'm sorry I haven't been able to get a foot on the ladder

I'm sorry I self sabotage

I'm sorry I struggled through my teenage years

I'm sorry I don't like having my photo taken

I'm sorry about my overdraft

I'm sorry I had to borrow money from friends

I'm sorry I can't afford to go away

I'm sorry I can't cook

I'm sorry I don't feel comfortable undressing in front of you

I'm sorry my hip hurts when I try and run

I'm sorry I frittered away my opportunities

I'm sorry I speak no languages other than English

I'm sorry my dyslexia makes reading difficult for me

I'm sorry I can't swim well

I'm sorry I don't like going out in the heat

I'm sorry my bathroom has mould on the shower

I'm sorry my future is hazy

I'm sorry I'm so susceptible to ear infections in winter

I'm sorry my high degree myopia makes me anxious in crowded spaces

I'm sorry I can't drive

I'm sorry I get out of breath going up the stairs

I'm sorry I don't have a lot of friends

I'm sorry I never believe you when you pay me a compliment

I'm sorry coffee makes my hands shake

I'm sorry I don't like complex flavours

I'm sorry I'm not hardy

I'm sorry I'm not adventurous

I'm sorry that I don't go shopping often

I'm sorry I don't like trying on clothes

I'm sorry I'm disconnected from current affairs

I'm sorry I don't fully comprehend the whole situation sometimes

I'm sorry I don't have a skill or a craft

I'm sorry that I procrastinate

I'm sorry there's a void in me

I'm sorry I have no purpose

I'm sorry that I'm not always mindful of my decisions

I'm sorry that I remain sitting for extended periods

I'm sorry that my body is disgusting

That my hygiene isn't good

That my genitals are repellant

     Mmn

I wish things were different

I wish they didn't exist

I wish I could cut them off–

     Say that again–

That's what I'd do if I could–

     Go on–

Take the scissors from the drawer–

Cut them out and leave an empty space

Without presence– without feeling–

     Keep going–

Cut off my stupid hair

Cut off my nails

Cut off my fingers

Cut off my toes

Cut off my hands and feet– my arms and legs–

Cut from here– at the base of my abdomen–

Through the skin and the yellow grey fat– the undeveloped muscles–

Right up through the centre of my chest– through the sternum to the neck– through the centre of my face–

Allow myself to open up– like the bud of a flower–

Lift out my heart and stomach and lungs–

Lift out my digestive tract–

Lift out handfuls of rotten leaves–

Of broken branches–

Of stagnant pulp–

Lay it all out for you to look at– to examine–

Push the blades of the scissors into my exposed brain and cut out all the negative thoughts– all the bad memories– all the misgivings– all the self awareness– all the pity and the doubt– all the fear and the uncertainty– all the sickness and the weakness and the failings and the sorrow– cut them out of me– cut them out and chop them up into tiny pieces–

Chop them up with the rest of me—

Chop them up until they disappear—

Until I disappear— until I don't exist—

Is this too much—?

Am I oversharing—?

Or is this good—?

No, this is good

Someone– not you– reaches down into the sand. They pull out a key

It's not too late– you know that don't you–?

It's never too late–

Nothing is impossible

Impossible is nothing

You are not immutable

You are a work in progress

You regenerate in every moment

Every new moment is filled with possibility

The possibility of change–

It's down to you

It's all down to you

You

You

You

Yes you

You and you alone

You're the catalyst

You're the stimulant

The ball's in your court

You're the master of your own destiny

Be the change you want to see in the world

> *You dig in the sand until you find a key. You lift it up and examine it—*
> *You dig until you find another— and another—*
> *The sand is full of keys— each one different.*
> *You look down at the keys in your hands.*

You're as fluid as water

You're as clear as the mountain spring

You flow over the dark rocks

Between the conifers

You fill up the spaces

You seep down into the earth

You soak into the roots

You unfurl leaves

Breathe

Breathe in

Breathe deep

Keep your eyes closed

Feel yourself expanding

You're everywhere

You're everything

You're anything you want to be

You have options

You have choices

You're not definitive

You're not conclusive

You're the infinite sky

You're the clouds forming

You're the light behind the clouds

You're the air you breathe

You're the ground under your feet

You're the branches reaching out

You're pushing through the branches

You're in constant motion

You're on a journey

You come to a clearing– to the edge of a lake

You're looking down into the water

Underneath–

Beyond the surface–

Behind the curvature of the pupil–

Deep in the black pool–

There I am

The true you

The true me

Down at the bottom

Reaching out–

Reaching out through the eyes– look–

The outstretched fingers– the hands– the arms appearing–

Can you see those arms–?

Arms that really fill the sleeve–

Arms that are capable of lifting so much–

So much cast iron–

Can you see the well proportioned leg–?

The firm hamstring–

Kicking through the water–

Pushing me forward–

The soft foot pointed

The nails neatly filed—

Neatly painted even—

Look how the colour suits my skin tone—

The skin exfoliated—

Moisturised—

Clear—

The hair conditioned—

Can you see this perfect hair—?

Perfectly groomed

Perfectly groomed hair on my head and between my legs

Matching my face shape

Accentuating my genitals

Shaped and styled by a professional—

Look at me stretching out in expensive neon activewear

Muscles lithe under my dark skin

Deep dark purple black

Brown

Beige

Peach

Ivory

Porcelain

Gentle bone china white–

See me glisten with perspiration–

Sweat running down between taut pectorals–

Between ample cleavage–

See the slim waist–

Hourglass figure–

Inverted triangle–

See me lifting the weighted ball

Pushing the bar

Holding myself up

Running my hands through my thick chest hair–

Deep into my professionally shaped beard– yes– if I want to–

Or over the freshly waxed abdominals– if that's what I prefer–

The freshly waxed legs–

The swimmer's body

Well proportioned

Washboard stomach

Floating

Flexed

Ab crack

V cut

Thigh gap

Groin bulging

Cleavage heaving

Anus bleached

Lungs breathing fresh air

Deep fresh clean air

Drinking pure water

Drinking electrolytes

Eating clean

Eating fresh fruit

Freshly plucked from the trees

Running

Sprinting

Toe off

Mid flight

Leg lifted

Legs open

Heart open

Chest open

Assertive

Fierce

Determined

Self determined

Sideways splits

Square jaw

Oval face

Triumphant smile

Five hundred pound deadlift

Crewcut

High pony

Golden waves

Tight black curls

Short back and sides

Auburn crop

Clean shave

Severe bob

Bedhead

Designer stubble

There you are and there you are and there you are and there
you are

You could slip through a keyhole

Under a fence

Step over a building

You're all greased up

Your body oiled

Glistening look–

Slippery

Wet

Wrestling look–

Wrestling on a tarpaulin

Opponent between your thighs

Eyes wide

You're strong

You're powerful

You're winning

Look at my compression shorts

Look at my wireless headphones

Look at my trainers

Made from bright durable nylon mesh

With flexible polyurethane soles

Look at my leggings

My curves

My bulk

Look at me in silk

In denim

In flannel

Look at my boots

Look at the grip

Look at this heel

Look at me in all black

Offset with gold jewellery

Look at the cut of this jacket

Look at this shirt

Look at the way the fabric falls

Look at the swoosh

Look at the three stripes

Look at this print

Look at this pattern

Look at me in tights

Look at me in form fitting underwear

Look at me naked

Look at me bending over

Look at me flex

Look at me owning it

Look at my poise

Silhouetted against the sunset

Look at my swimwear

Polybutylene terephthalate

Tight against my skin

Look at my inner strength

Look how my inner strength is reflected through my poise

Leg lifted up behind me

Arms over my head

My hands interlinked around my ankle

My head up

Eyes fixed

Deep back bend

Natarajasana

Look where I've been

Look at all the places where I've been

Look at me scaling this mountain

Look at me on the edge of this canyon

Look at me sitting on this rock

Look at me taking in the vista in the hazy evening light

Look how receptive I am to its transient beauty

I'm at peace

My mind is clear

Yes–

Even in this angry world

This bitter rock

This infinite vacuum

This meaningless void

Look how I rise above

Look how I accept what I don't understand

Look at the purity of my acceptance

My mind is an oasis

My mind is a blue sky

My mind is a tranquil ocean

The water is clear

The water is inviting

Dive in

Let me flood round your imperfect body

Your broken heart

Let me pull you under

Shape your outline

Stretch you out

Lift your legs

Cleanse your skin

Soak through you

Rush cold into your open mouth

We know that you're in pain

We know that you're suffering

We know that you've been crying

There's no need to be ashamed– not of your tears

In fact your unhappiness– the expulsion of water from your red raw eyes– is an important part of your journey–

At the heart of every crystal drop is an understanding that something has to change–

Your current failings

Your shortcomings

Your inadequacies

Have come to teach you something

Have come to propel you forward

Onward into the future

Open the curtains– the sun is lifting–

The light streaming orange through the dirty glass–

See the line cut across the room–

It touches your skin– your feet stand in it–

Take the used plates and put them in the sink

Pour away the mould from the top of the tea

Bring down the laundry and put it in the machine

That's all it takes–

Make a choice–

Make a promise with yourself–

Make your bed with clean sheets–

Throw away the grey t-shirt–

The cheap underwear–

The worn out shoes–

The old jogging bottoms–

Anything that's ripped or stained—

They belong to the old you—

The not good enough you—

Reject that person— those thoughts—

Consign them to history—

To the dustbin with the rubbish—

The used dishcloths—

The empty packaging—

The half eaten food—

The crusts

The bones

The dust

The teabags

You stand on the precipice— balanced between two moments—

On the cusp of something amazing—

This is the end—

This is the beginning—

You're starting from here

You're starting from now

A large bin appears

Get in the bin

Get in the bin

Get in the bin

Get in the bin

You crawl into the bin and disappear
You vanish into the infinite void

The void
The void
The void
The void

In brand-new exercise clothes:

High knees–

That's it!

Don't stop!

Up

Up

Up

Up

Push off with the other foot

You should be lifting right off the floor

Straight into mountain climbers!

Plank position!

Bum down–

Engage your core–

Keep up the momentum–

One

Two

One

Two

100%

110

Don't slow down–!

You can't afford to slow down–

Do you want this to be a depressing story?

Do you want this to be a story about one of life's losers–?

Is that what you want?

Is that what you are?

I'm asking you–!

Answer me!

    No

Louder–!

    No–!

Jump forwards–

Burpees!

You're trying to touch the ceiling

Squat down–

Feet out–

Press up–

Elbows in– good

Chest to the floor– nice

Feet back–

Up to the ceiling!

Jump!

Make this a transformation story!

The kind of story people like!

An example of what you can achieve if you just

Kettlebells

Kettlebells

Come on!

Right up

Lift it

Lift it

Lift

Feel those arms burning

You're a good person

You're a good person

Say it

     I'm a good person

You deserve to be healthy

     I deserve to be healthy

You deserve a fit body

     I deserve a fit body

You deserve to love yourself

     I deserve to love myself

You're affecting change

     I'm affecting change

Summer's coming!

     Summer's coming–

You're going to be lying on a beach this summer

You're going to be in your swimwear

You're going to be on display–

Laid out in the sand– skin against the ground down rocks– your body burning in the heat–

What do you want people to think?

What conclusions do you want them to have when they see you–?

Keep hold of those weights!

Don't put the weights down!

Goblet squats–!

Steady rhythm

Down

Up

Down

Up

Deeper

Right down

Hold it

Hold it

Nice

Keep holding!

You're in charge of your own destiny!

Say it–!

     I'm in charge of my own destiny

Nobody has control over you!

     Nobody has control over me

You are on a journey!

I am on a journey!

The journey is your life!

The journey is my life–!

No one will derail your story!

No one will derail my story

You are in command of your own narrative!

I am in command of my own narrative

You shape who you are

I shape who I am

You choose what you become

I choose what I become

This is about you

This is about me

You

Me

You

Me

You

You

You

You

Me

Me

Me

Me

Me

Me

Me

Me

Me

Me

Me

I will not give in

I will not be complacent

I will not lose focus

I will not stop persevering

I will not make excuses

I will not blame others for my own shortcomings

I will not ask for a leg up

I will not be tied down

I will not ask you to be there for me

I will not feel obligated

I will not hold your hand

I will not sympathise

I will not see your suffering and I will not ask you to see mine

I will not soften my resolve

I will not give up my seat

I will not give up my time

I will tap my watch when I want to leave

I will not volunteer–

I will not work for nothing– why should I?

I will not share my spoils

I will not pay tax if I can avoid it

I will not capitulate to beggars

I will not see your heartache

I will not dignify you with a response

I will not look at old photos

I will not visit you if you move away

I will not reconnect with lost lovers

I will not offer support

I will not change nappies

I will not sit beside my mother on her deathbed

I will not be blamed for someone else's failures

I will not console you in your self pity

I will offer no condolences nor send any cards

I will focus on myself

I will develop my own unique strengths

I will eradicate my weaknesses

I will better myself in all areas

I will utilise my voice

I will focus on compound lifts

I will be open to new experiences

I will be in a constant state of readiness

I will weigh individual portions of almonds

I will monitor the number of steps I take daily

I will keep track of my calorie intake

I will photograph myself doing a handstand and share it

I will make the most of what I have available

I will only donate to charitable causes I believe in

I will lead by example

I'll make the most of my assets

I'll monetise my skills

I'll work overtime if I have to

I will work hard and enjoy the fruits of my labour

I will enjoy the wonderful sweet crunch of the apples of my labour

Because I earned them

I earned these apples

The apples of life

I earned each bite

I earned every pleasurable moment

I deserve them

I deserve every drop of sweet juice

I'll immerse myself in it—

In life's multifaceted joys

I'll soak up every moment

Look—

Look how I'm sweating—

Look at the sweat dripping from me—

Taste it—

Each drop of sweat is testament to my labour

A dance—

    The dance becomes beautiful

    The dance becomes hypnotic

    The dance goes on and on

A song—

        Breathe in deep
        Maximise oxygen intake

        Push yourself
        Monitor increasing heart rate

        Work your body
        Release adenosine triphosphate

        Capillaries dilating
        Heat dissipating

        At the anaerobic threshold
        Lactic acid takes hold

        Microtrauma in the cells
        Hypertrophy of muscles

        Breathe in deep

        Push yourself

        Work your body

The song and the dance are separate, although can overlap

Somebody is cutting pictures out of magazines and putting them in a folder. Everyone wears a key around their neck. A small box somewhere.

We love what you're doing

We love the message you send out to people

It's such a positive message

We love a positive message

We love a success story–

Success stories are aspirational

You're aspirational

We love what you stand for

We love your truthfulness

We love your authenticity

We love your resolve

We love your determination

We love your photographs

We love your writing

We love your videos

We love the way you've really embraced social media

We love the way you've used it to tell your own story

We think you're so brave

We know the strength it takes to put yourself out there

To put those photographs of yourself on the internet

Those photographs of yourself looking so hideous

Those photographs of your body at its worst

That takes real courage

But it's so incredibly positive

It's so incredibly normalising

It's actually incredibly empowering– to see someone doing that–

To see someone taking control of that situation–

To see someone tackling it head on and winning–

Because you look astonishing now

Do you mind if we say that?

We think you look astonishing

Attractive even–

Yes attractive

Clearly attractive–

Lots of people here are attracted to you

We whisper actually– when you come in the room

We nudge each other

We talk about you over our morning coffee

At lunch time

In the pub after work

What a change! we say–

What a transformation!

You're like a different person!

Even your face has changed–!

Your skin is a different colour

Your features are more pronounced

Your cheekbones

Your jawline

Although of course it's not just your new appearance that we find attractive– it's the fact that you've been on this journey– it's the fact that you were determined enough to make it happen for yourself– because everybody talks– everybody has dreams– but talk is cheap– dreams are abstract–; you took real, tangible action–

That's an incredibly attractive characteristic!

With your solid fanbase–

With your improving physique–

With your backstory–

We really think we can make this work–

We think this is an excellent opportunity

We assume you want to keep growing–

Of course you do– don't you?– who doesn't?

Growth– progress– development– momentum–

Especially when there's the prospect of hard cash on the table–

Would you like a drink by the way?

We can get you a drink–

Water–?

Or sparkling water–?

We've got sparkling water on tap here–

> *A glass of water is brought in– it sparkles.*
> *You drink it all.   You need it.*

We can manage your schedule–

We can help you with your branding–

We can develop your website–

We can help you maximise your online presence– get you in people's search results– increase your output–

We have writers here that are able to mimic your own unique voice–

We can generate more content that way–

We would aim to double your followers in six to eight months–

That's a modest projection of what we think we can achieve–

We can do detailed research into the demographic of your fanbase—

We can help you expand into new areas—

We have access to some exceptional people in some incredible companies

We know they would be keen to have you promoting their brands

We can work with you to carefully curate the brands you promote

We can increase your press coverage

We've got good press contacts here

We can get them freebies and they love the freebies!

We take them out for dinner

We give them complimentary trainers

Coats

Tickets

Weekends away—

They'll pretty much write what we tell them to

That's an exaggeration of course—

The press is independent—

But we get final sign off on most of the articles

We can get you TV spots—

Paid public appearances—

We've worked with most of the major publishers to produce a number of bestselling hardbacks

We can ensure you keep making improvements to your figure

We can get you working with a personal trainer

We can have some professional photos taken

We can put together a small team to work on your videos with you

We can help augment the revenue from those

We can get you a dedicated stylist

We can develop your own signature look

We can gently push towards a more fashion forward approach

We can give you a new haircut

Improve the growth in thinning areas

Move the follicles from the back of your neck

Get rid of any greys

We can provide you with high end personal care products–

Moisturiser–

Hand cream–

Facial toner–

Lip balm–

We can get your teeth whitened

Straighten them out–

Improve your body shape by shooting from certain angles

Eradicate minor deficiencies in post

Cover unsightly blemishes with make up

We can get your excess skin removed

Inject your veins with sclerosant

Inject your lips with fat

Numb your facial muscles to minimise creasing

We can help you manage the psychological side effects of the changes you've been through

We have experts on hand who can break down the thinking behind stress or anxiety–

Help you manage loneliness– provide coping mechanisms–

Provide a safe space to explore negative thoughts–

We can alter your hormones–

We can manage the way you see yourself–

We can improve your serotonin uptake–

We want you to be happy–

Looking happy, exactly–

Of course we do–

People like happy–

Happy is good–

Someone– not you– removes the key from their neck. It opens the small box. Inside the small box is another key; this one is special somehow.

A large mirrored cube is brought in. The special key slots into the keyhole.

The box opens– inside is a miniature sized idyllic glade. You go up to the glade inside the cube and look at it. The glade is completely real– beautiful and miraculous.

I saw your blog, you say–

I loved reading your blog–

I followed you online obviously– on various platforms–

I watched the videos you posted on social media–

The videos were so inspiring–

I saw you on a poster– on a number of posters– and not just small or medium sized posters– huge posters, stretched on the side of buildings–

I saw you on television selling health products–

On chat shows–

On charity fundraisers– making cameo appearances–

I saw you in magazines– I read interviews–

I used the products you endorsed– because I trusted your judgement–

I bought your book as well– yes– you laugh–

I made all the recipes– I started at the beginning and worked my way through–

I read it over and over until all the pages fell out– I had to buy another copy!

I came to one of your book signings– do you remember?

I had to queue in the rain–

I camped out overnight– that's how desperate I was to meet you–

I slept on the street– lots of us did–

We slept on the pavements in sacks–

We brought gifts to give you– I– for instance– brought you a drawing I had done– because I was good at drawing– a drawing of you– and you said it was an incredible likeness– do you remember?

You didn't disappoint me–

You smiled graciously–

You took a photo with me–

My heart ached, you said–

My heart ached when I saw you–

I wanted to be you–

I wanted to be inside you–

Just have a part of you that I could curl up inside forever–

And there were tears in your eyes now– at the thought of that–

Milk white pearls rolling down your cheeks–

You put your arm around me, you said, and I felt your power–

You were there beside me and I felt your strength of spirit—

I felt your worth—

I felt your value—

Look

Look

Look

Look

Look

Look at my drawing, you said, of you— of you standing in the sunshine—

Your hands were shaking—

It was an incredible likeness

A transformation takes place.

And another.

And another.

And another.

I haven't always looked like this– I haven't always been in this position– a lot of people look me up– see my recipes– my exercise videos– my daily vlogs– my current life– my new home– but without the context of my personal journey–

The people who've been with me since the beginning– they know the effort and the dedication I've put into getting to this point– and I think that context is really important–

Because fitness isn't given– fitness– like anything– is earned–

it's earned in incremental steps– and it isn't always easy–

it isn't always easy to stick to your plan–

your diet–

if you're ill maybe– if you're feeling tired after work–

if it's raining outside–

I understand that

I understand it because I've felt it myself

And that's what I wanted to share in the book–

Because when people are able to visualise the full arc of my journey it inspires them–

They realise that yes– dreams can come true– that the opportunities are out there– even for them– on the simple proviso that they make the right choices– choices about what they eat for example– about what they do– about how they spend their time–

All they have to do is keep making those choices– every single day–

And that's actually a very empowering message when you think about it–

Because those choices are up to you–

They're within your control as an individual–

I didn't just wake up like this– there isn't some special innate characteristic that I have within me–

I decided to look like this–

I decided to be like this– and you can too–

Because what makes me special is not what I am but what I do–

And that means everyone– each and every one of you– you all have the ability to be as remarkable and beautiful as I am–

You all have that power and strength within you–

So if you're sitting there– if you're watching and you're thinking– I'm not happy– not happy with my life– with my situation– with my body– with where I'm at right now– I'm here to say– you can change that– any of it– all of it even– starting today–

You can unwrap yourself from a packet at anytime– in every moment– right now if you want to– and suddenly you're as good as new–

I'm living proof of that– living, breathing proof–

And the book makes it easy–

The book has a very clear and concise 12 Month Plan

The recipes are delicious–

They're incredibly delicious–

People have this idea that healthy food doesn't taste good– or shouldn't taste good–

But these recipes totally disprove that fallacy–

What's great– for me– about the recipes in the book– and the workouts in fact–

Yes we should mention the workouts–!

Twenty minute daily workouts–

What's twenty minutes–?

We can all spare twenty minutes–

They're not complicated–

No–

They're very manageable–

For beginners–

For people who might not have an incredible amount of skill or time or ability–

For ordinary people–

Exactly– ordinary everyday working people–

Because the right choices aren't necessarily technically difficult–

That's right–

They're within reach–

You don't have to be an athlete to exercise–

You don't have to be a chef to eat healthily– if you can cut up a carrot–

You don't even have to cut up a carrot– you can buy pre-cut carrot– that's something you say, don't you?

There's no shame in buying a pre-cut carrot– carrot batons–

Pre-cut carrot batons are still carrot–

But I think that's important– because you know– most of the time when I open a recipe book– most recipe books– I look at the pictures and think that looks appetising– my mouth waters– but then I look at the writing–

Yes you look at the writing–

It's true!

And think– oh no– I couldn't make that– I can't even make sense of that– all that writing– that size 8 font– plus then you've got to have specialist equipment– a piping bag for example, or a muslin cloth– and it's got to simmer all day– or roast for hours– or rest–

Rest–!

People have jobs!

People have children!

People want to come home– I want to come home–

They don't want to use a piping bag!

No!

The fact you can throw something together in under twenty minutes

Something that's healthy!

Something that uses simple, accessible ingredients–

Ingredients you can pick up in your local supermarket–

It's a recipe book for people who don't buy recipe books!

And if you stick with it– if you keep going– that's what you're saying isn't it–? and it's true– then maybe you can become that top chef or that incredible athlete that other people look up to–

Applause

Applause becomes clapping–
The clapping becomes steady, a rhythm–
Then more complex– musical.
This continues for a long time, until eventually the clapping becomes applause again.

So tell us– are you in a relationship at the moment–?

Because you've very eligible–

Haha

Hahaha

No but seriously–

Haha

No I'm not currently in a relationship no

Not per. se– not in the traditional sense– because you know– I'm very busy at the moment–

I'm travelling a lot for work– I have to travel a lot–

It's not possible to commit to a single person when you're always travelling

But I see people– there are people that I see–

People plural–?

Yes–

That's great–!

That's amazing!

So you're well satiated–?

Yes– haha– although I'm always in the market to meet new people–!

You can never have too much of a good thing!

No–!

That's what I believe–!

Do people approach you?

Does that bother you if they approach you–?

I love it when people approach me–

What kind of person do you go for–?

Do you have a type?

No I'm not restrictive–

I try to stay welcoming to all experiences– in terms of ethnicity– in terms of age– in terms of gender–

I love that–

That's beautiful

It's always better to say yes– isn't it?

Yes–

Yes–!

Yes opens doors

That's so true!

Although there are certain characteristics that I value–

I prefer fit and healthy people obviously– people who are energetic–

People who look after their bodies–

People with that inner glow– who are equally open minded–

People burning with ferocity and beauty

People with a well placed belief in their ability

People who like to keep things fresh

People who aren't looking for anything permanent

People who understand where I'm at right now and respect that–

People who aren't going to get weird

People with different modes of being

People who want to have a bit of fun

People who aren't afraid of role play, for instance

People who know how to dress for an occasion

People who are free–

Something happens here

My followers know that I moved to a new flat recently–
a beautiful new flat– you've probably seen the pictures–

With a floor to ceiling window that overlooks the city–

I worked with an interior design specialist–

And one of the things we did was install a statement mirror in
the bedroom– six foot by twelve– which leans against the wall
opposite the bed– because when I'm making love– can I say
this–?

Of course!

You can say whatever you want–

You're entitled to–

We want to hear it–!

When I'm with my lover– or lovers– in my freshly washed
sheets– skin vivid against the crisp white–

When they're pressing up against me– fingers in my hair–
teeth round my arm– my hardened nipple– for example–

When their breath is in my ear– when they're scratching my
back– pushing a finger in my mouth– or vice versa– when my
finger is in theirs– their lips around it–

When they're pushing back against the headboard– or
grasping my obliques for better traction–

When I'm grabbing at their swollen genitals– shaved and hot
and swollen– and they're grabbing at mine–

When our genitals intermingle– when there's lubricant
running down our legs– you know?

When they're opening their mouth to receive my wet throbbing crotch–

Opening eagerly– with desperate desire– slurping wet desire–

When I'm sticking my tongue deep into their prised opened anus– tracing the rim of it– each ridge–

When they're pushing a thumb inside me– or a plastic toy– or a string of steel beads–

When they're pulling it out again–

When there's pleasure surging through me–

I love to look up and see myself– see my body in the mirror–

The curved lines– the well defined edges–

Immaculate and vivid–

See each rhythmical thrust– see us grinding steadily– see the arched backs–

See my heaving chest–

See my muscle groups working–

Look at me– behind the glass– on the bed– in the bedroom reflected there–

Look at my life–

Look at my body–

It's so unreal–

So receptive–

So desirable–

So desired–

So full of possibility–

I can almost reach out and touch it–

Look at them–

Look how much they want it–

Yes they want it–

Look at their eyes–

Their eyes are wide open

Their eyes are looking at me– they're looking at me in the mirror–

Looking at themselves in relation to me–

The light refracting off the surface of my skin– onto the glass–
into the black pool– onto the surface of the retina–

Our bodies expanding into the air around us–

Something happens here

After we've finished we lie back breathing–

We don't speak– I mean ideally

Ideally nobody speaks– it's just easier isn't it–? you probably
agree–

We have nothing to say to each other anyway– not really–

We just shower to wash away the dried spit and cum from our
bodies

The sweat

Towel down with a fresh towel and dress and then they step into a cab– turn sideways and vanish– which suits them and suits me–

Suits us all just fine

Because you know– I'm busy– they're busy– we're all busy people

We don't have the time– as you say– to chop up a carrot, let alone make small talk

When they've gone I'll grab a snack usually–

Maybe a bowl of cereal or some dried fruit

Go to the window–

Look out at the sunset–

The clouds folding into each other–

The violet sky–

The buildings silhouetted on the distant horizon–

The lights are on in the buildings–

The silver river ebbs below–

The cars crawl–

The people are tiny dots– long shadows–

You're so far removed from them– they're unreal almost–

They're like figments of your imagination–

I catch up on my notifications– send out some replies–

Do a few bodyweight exercises

Some compound lifts

Weigh myself and log it

Calculate my body fat percentage

Take photos– front and side

Feel the air against my skin

The temperature controlled air

I clean my teeth

The room is silent

The glass is triple glazed

Good–

I get into bed

My eyes are open

My body aches

Tomorrow is another day

Can you come forward–?

Come to the front–

Come to the front for this bit–

Don't look at us—

You can't see us—

We're invisible—

We don't exist—

You're not here with us—

You're somewhere else entirely

Look up there— see the mark— that's your focus—

You're walking towards that—

You're thinking of something— something only you know about— something that we're not privy to— that we don't understand—

That we couldn't even possibly begin to understand—

Take a step towards it

That's it—

And again— good

Keep going

> *You take a step forward; and another; and another; and another; and another. You don't move from the spot.*

> *Something happens here.*

I'm moving steadily– one foot in front of the other– towards a shape on the horizon–

The sun is beginning to rise– inching upwards in front of me–

How long have I been walking–?

How many days–?

My feet are blistered–

My legs are sore

I have a key around my neck

By midday the sky is white– shimmering air distorts the ground–

It's too hot to move–

There's nowhere to hide out here– no trees– no buildings– no clouds–

Just sand in all directions– sand and sand and sand–

I build a canopy to shelter from the heat

I'm used to building it now–

Two layers of canvas held taut between four wooden poles–

My hands move automatically– tie the ropes at the corners– hammer the pegs into the ground–

I'm sweating– my throat is dry–

I sit under it– keep my head down– avoiding the glare of the light– keeping still while the day passes over–

I drink from the plastic bottle I have with me– the water is thick and warm– it's almost finished–

I'm breathing gently–

When it is cool enough I dismantle the shelter– pack it up– lift it onto my back– keep going–

The temperature drops with the sun– becomes cold even– it's a relief–

I unwrap the scarf from round my head– bare my arms– my skin contracts–

I stop moving at dusk and set up a bed for myself–

I eat a few mouthfuls of bread– sip at the water– tiny sips–

My lips are cracked– my face is burned–

I want to drink it all but I need to preserve it

I lie back and look up–

The sand supports me–

The stars are out–

The air is still–

The world turns on its axis–

Here I am–

This is me–

Sleep

Sleep

Sleep

Light encroaches over the horizon again–

Before the sun reappears I pack up my bed– put it on my
back– drink what I have left– not even a mouthful– and
shuffle slowly onward–

What will happen to me today, I think– with nothing left to
drink–?

I could just lie down–

I could just lie down and stop– give up–

But I keep moving forward– something propels me steadily
towards the shape on the horizon– is it getting closer–? I can't tell–

I picture myself there– at the shape– whatever it is–

Finding the remains of collapsed stone pillars–

Moving between them slowly–

Large rocks cut into squares lie half buried–

Large rocks with patterns carved into them–

I close my eyes–

My fingers trace the grooves–

When I brush away the sand I find depictions of people–
drawings in profile or facing outward–

They stand beside patterns that curve like waves– a riverbank–

There are plants– a bird– animals–

There are people washing themselves–

There are people swimming–

There's a statue– twelve feet high– leaning at an angle–

Oddly proportioned– primitive– arms out in front–

There's an empty bowl in the hands– the thumbs are missing but the fingers remain– an approximation of fingernails even–

The head is fixed– looking forward– a shawl worn over the hair– stopping at the shoulder– the face eroded– the nose broken off– the left side concave–

I lift my own hands up against it–

The stone is hard but grain by grain the wind carries it away until it vanishes–

There's nothing left–

I give up–

My knees collapse with exhaustion–

I'm dehydrated and fatigued–

This is the end–

This is the end–

I keep my eyes closed–

Something protrudes from the ground–

A corner–

The sand gives way to reveal a wooden chest– half buried–

I dig around it and find a handle– pull it free from the earth
with a struggle–

On the chest are more primitive figures–

Figures painted in gold– drinking from small urns–

The chest is locked but I still have the key around my neck

This, I think, is the key for this lock–

I know it in my bones–

I lift it over my head–

It fits inside– yes– fits in the slot perfectly– but won't turn–
maybe it's too old– broken– maybe it's full of sand–

I twist harder– still nothing–

I need to get inside– the contents are mine–

I look around– take a rock from the ground– raise it up–

I'm weak but the lock breaks in one and I flip back the lid–

Inside the chest are ice cubes–

Perfect three dimensional squares of frozen water–

They glow white–

Water vapour rises up from them in slow curls–

And laid in the ice are bottles–

Bottles of soft drink–

I reach in to take one– expecting it to disappear between my fingers– a mirage–

But it's cold in my hand– smooth– wet– there is condensation on the glass– it's real– as real as I am–

I lift it up so you can see the logo–

Crack open the lid–

Crack– hiss– yes– the gentle release of air–

Hold it to my lips– tip it up–

The relief– oh– there it is– the relief

Air displaces the liquid– bubbles rise in the glass– the sun silhouettes me from behind– makes the bottle glow almost–

I drink and drink and drink

Liquid rushing down my throat–

This is life– here– in this moment–

Look–

See how it spreads through me–

Life–

Life–

Life–

How sweet it tastes–

You've broken through

You've risen above

There you are–

Yes– you're there look

You're more than human now

You're an idea

You're a principle

You're an asset

You're a benchmark

You're a cultural reference point

You're a saleable commodity

You're rich

You're talented

You're alive

You're more than alive– you're living

You're really living

A diamond cut and turning on a pedestal

Plants spring up– stems pushing through the grains of sand–

Green leaves unfurling–

Buds appear on the growing stems and crack open like hearts–
their gentle edges tender and raw with intensity–

Pink– yellow– blue pastel–

Tropical orange and purple–

Each pushing back to reveal themselves–

They cover the floor around me– and spread– moving outward–

The sand is obliterated by them– the dry air becomes humid–

Water rushes down– cascades over the dry rocks– beautiful
clear water– the colour of lapis lazuli–

It collects and pools at my feet– heals my blisters–

Palms push up at the edges– lean in gently– are reflected in
the surface–

Vines grow around the stems– parrots and toucans sit on the
branches–

Fluorescent butterflies flutter in front–

Hummingbirds poke into orchids–

A hippo rises from the lake– a crocodile lies on the bank–

A monkey swings behind me–

A lioness tends to her cubs–

Here I am within it–

My heart beating in unison with the hearts of the animals–

The flow of the water–

Drinking this soft drink–

This superfood–

It's low in calories–

It's naturally fat and cholesterol free–

It has more potassium than four bananas–

It's pure–

It's simple–

It's mother nature's sports drink

Raw organic coconut water–

It actively replenishes electrolytes after exercise

It comes in a stylish premium one hundred per cent recycled glass bottle

It's available in most major supermarkets

It's my go-to drink after a workout– or anytime in fact–

Anytime I need a quick burst of hydration–!

> *A bottle of Cocowater+ is brought on. You drink– however, the desert around you is not transformed.*
>
> *Another bottle is brought on. Again you drink; again no transformation.*
>
> *Another bottle. Again you drink; again no transformation.*

Another song–

Drink
Soft and sparkling flavours
Drink
Alternatives to milk

Drink
Distilled and filtered water
Drink
Freshly blended fruit

Drink
To stay hydrated
Drink
To stay alive

If you don't drink enough
Fluid you will die

Fluid body
Fluid mind

A New and Better You: a note on writing the show and my own personal process

Sometimes life takes you in unexpected directions.

My wife and I met whilst working together on a show at the Edinburgh festival and spent two joyous weeks drinking and immersing ourselves in contemporary culture. Before we knew it, five years had passed. We were married and had a son who was three. With a little help from our parents we relocated from London and bought a home outside York. Our future was mapped out in front of us.

But something was wrong.

My wife had stopped acting and worked in an office as an assistant. I called myself a writer but was not writing anything. Eight years had passed since my last play was produced. I was making about £12k a year copywriting for an online company.

I spent my days tidying the cupboards and washing crusty yoghurt from my son's clothes. I was not inspired. I had nothing interesting to write about. I used to look out of the window and I could sense the world was full of stories, but they were passing me by. My wife was always tired and my son would shout at a volume that was not conducive to creative thought.

On the eve of my thirtieth birthday I disclosed to my wife that I could no longer remain with her in that house. I had to climb through the window and go out into the world. I needed to be surrounded by strangers and strange stories – by unknown sights and smells. All I needed for my copywriting job was a laptop, which I packed into a suitcase and took with me on a plane to South-East Asia.

I threw away my mobile phone. I wanted to really be in the moment. I needed to feel like I existed again. I felt the dry earth between my fingers, the sun on my skin. I didn't speak the language but I felt an affinity with the people. I drifted for a year and experienced an awakening. I stood on beaches. I felt earthquakes. I tasted wonderful and exotic foods.

One night I had a dream. The previous week I had visited the Borobudur Temple Compounds – a UNESCO world heritage site – and now the Buddha came to me in my sleep. He was made of stone, but he showed me how the stone rippled like water. He spread himself into a deep pool and a lotus flowered on the surface. He let me step inside and I felt him wrap around my body like a shawl.

A vision came to me. I saw a shape unfurling in my mind, behind my eyes. A fissure in reality was slowly opening up. Geometric patterns folded into each other. I was on the boundary between two worlds. I was part of both of them. I was the door between them; a conduit. Messages from the other world passed through me. Time was not linear; progress was a myth; the societal norms of family and marriage were a construct; work was a prison that limited us. We needed to unhook ourselves; to free ourselves from the systematic oppression caused by the machinery of society – free ourselves to explore, to create, to exist, to discover – without expectation, without goals. Art was the answer – my art especially. My art was good.

For the first time in years I had something to say – an important message. Only I could tell it. It flowed out of me. Its relevance was astonishing. It was about the whole of civilisation; about humanity; about morality; about love and connection; about our relationship with each other and with the universe. It came from another place: a place of truth – not relative truth, but truth as clear and indisputable as a diamond. My process was a dance with the divine.

It is great to see this work being staged. It is great to be getting paid for writing this play – I deserve to be paid. It is great to see the actors' mouths open and close, to hear the words coming out – my words. I want these words to go into your ears. I want you to wake up like I did. I want you to see things in the same way I do. I want you to clap at the end – keep clapping – and acknowledge the depth of my insight; confirm in my heart the choices that I made to get here: the choice to follow my creative desires; the choice to stay active in the construction of my personal narrative; the choice to leave my wife and son standing in the doorway of that grey two bed terrace.

I now live with my new girlfriend in North London and am currently working on a pilot series for Channel 4. I am represented by Curtis Brown.

WWW.OBERONBOOKS.COM

Follow us on www.twitter.com/@oberonbooks
& www.facebook.com/OberonBooksLondon